# WHAT I LOVE ABOUT

# NAN

WRITTEN BY

_____

# ADDITIONAL FREE RESOURCES

Visit:
www.rocketstudiobooks.com/love

Get:
- Ideas & inspiration to make your book pop!
- A page of all the questions to draft your answers

## JOIN US ON INSTAGRAM
@LotusLovePress

# I LOVE IT WHEN WE

---

THANK YOU FOR TEACHING ME

_____

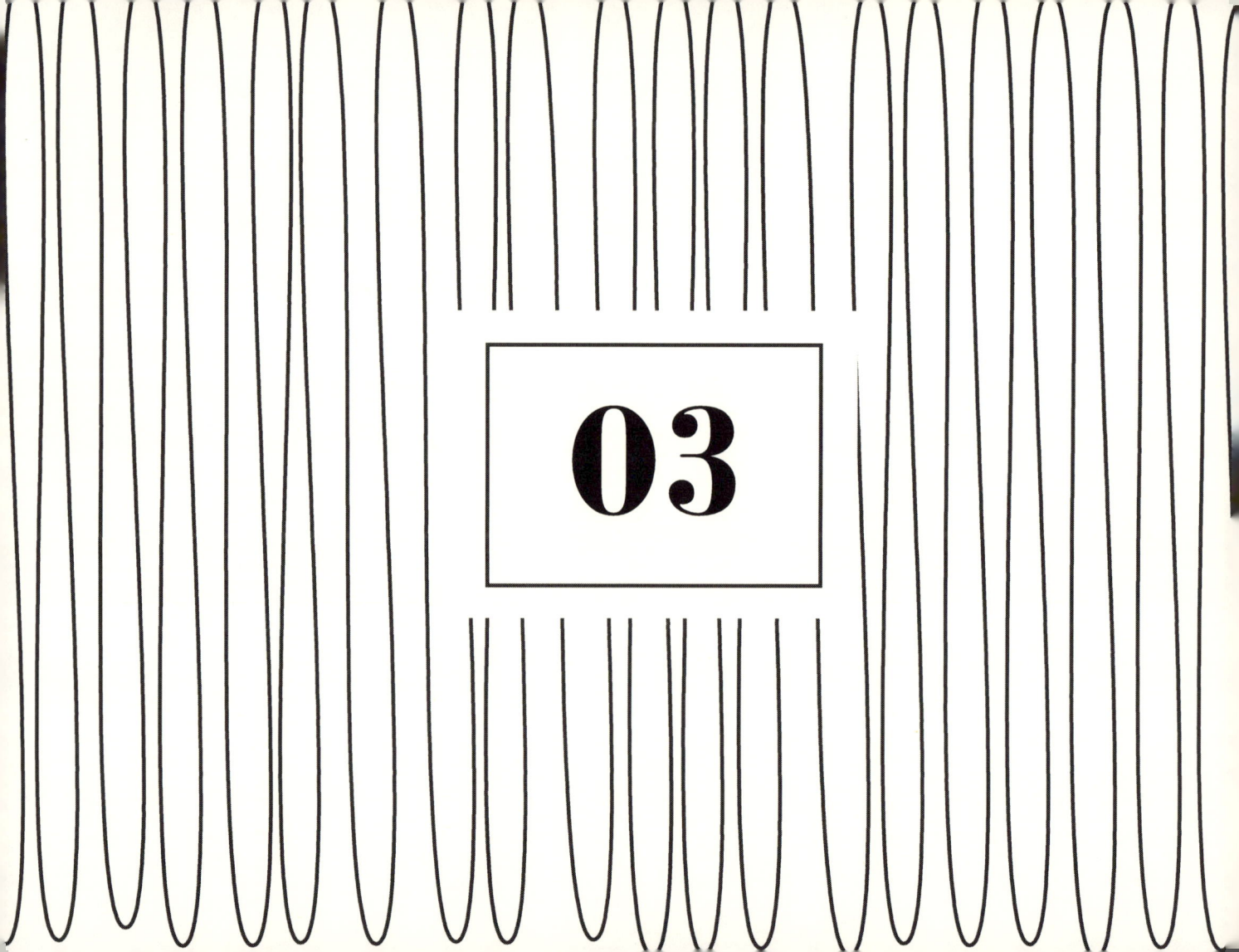

I KNOW YOU LOVE ME BECAUSE

_____

I LOVE HOW YOU ALWAYS

_____

THANK YOU FOR

_____

YOU ARE REALLY GOOD AT

_____

I LOVE IT WHEN YOU SAY

_____

IF YOU WERE AN ANIMAL, YOU'D BE

_____

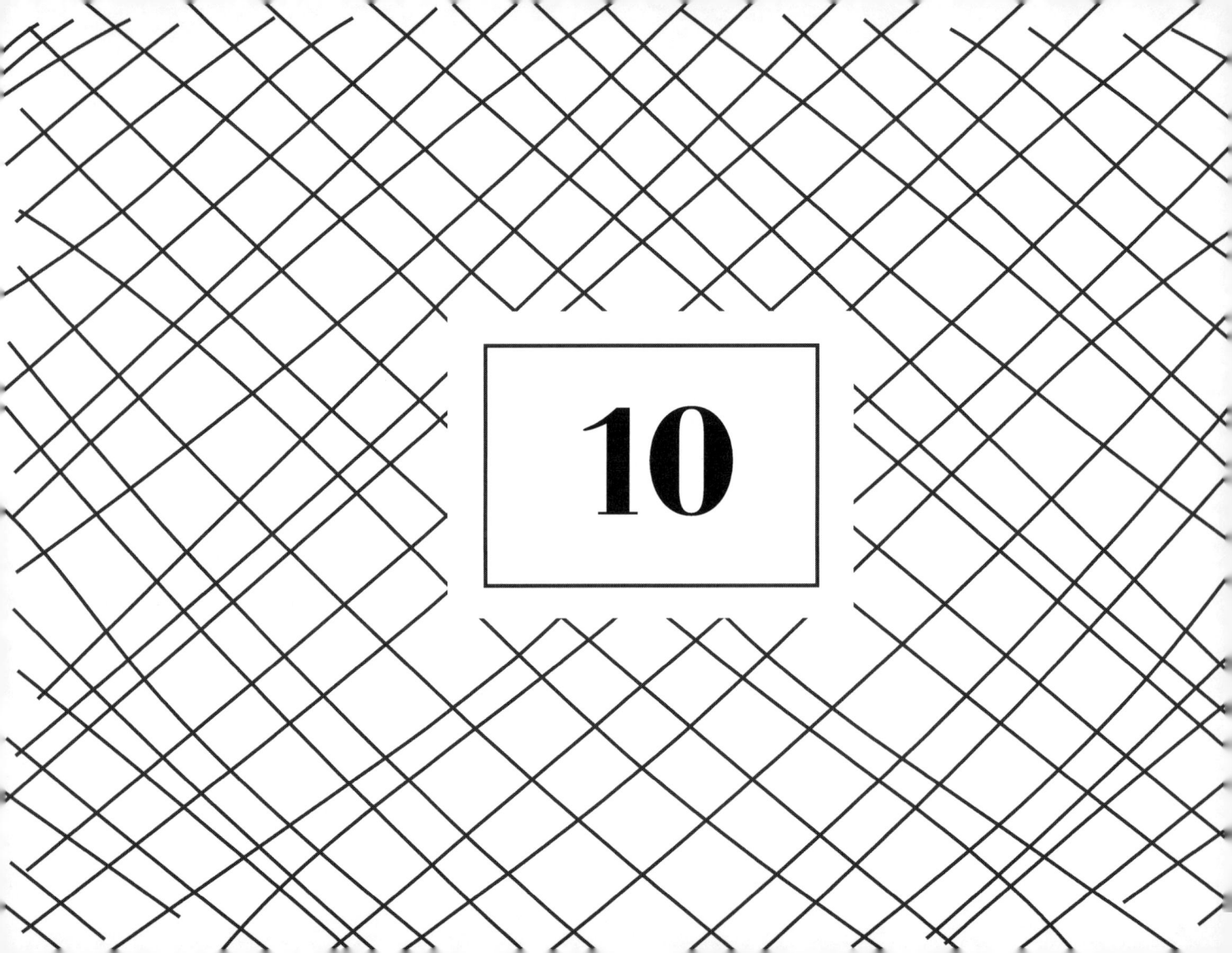

YOU MAKE ME LAUGH WHEN

_____

I'M GLAD WE

THE BEST THING ABOUT YOU IS

_____

YOU ARE BETTER THAN A

_____

YOU TAUGHT ME HOW TO

_____

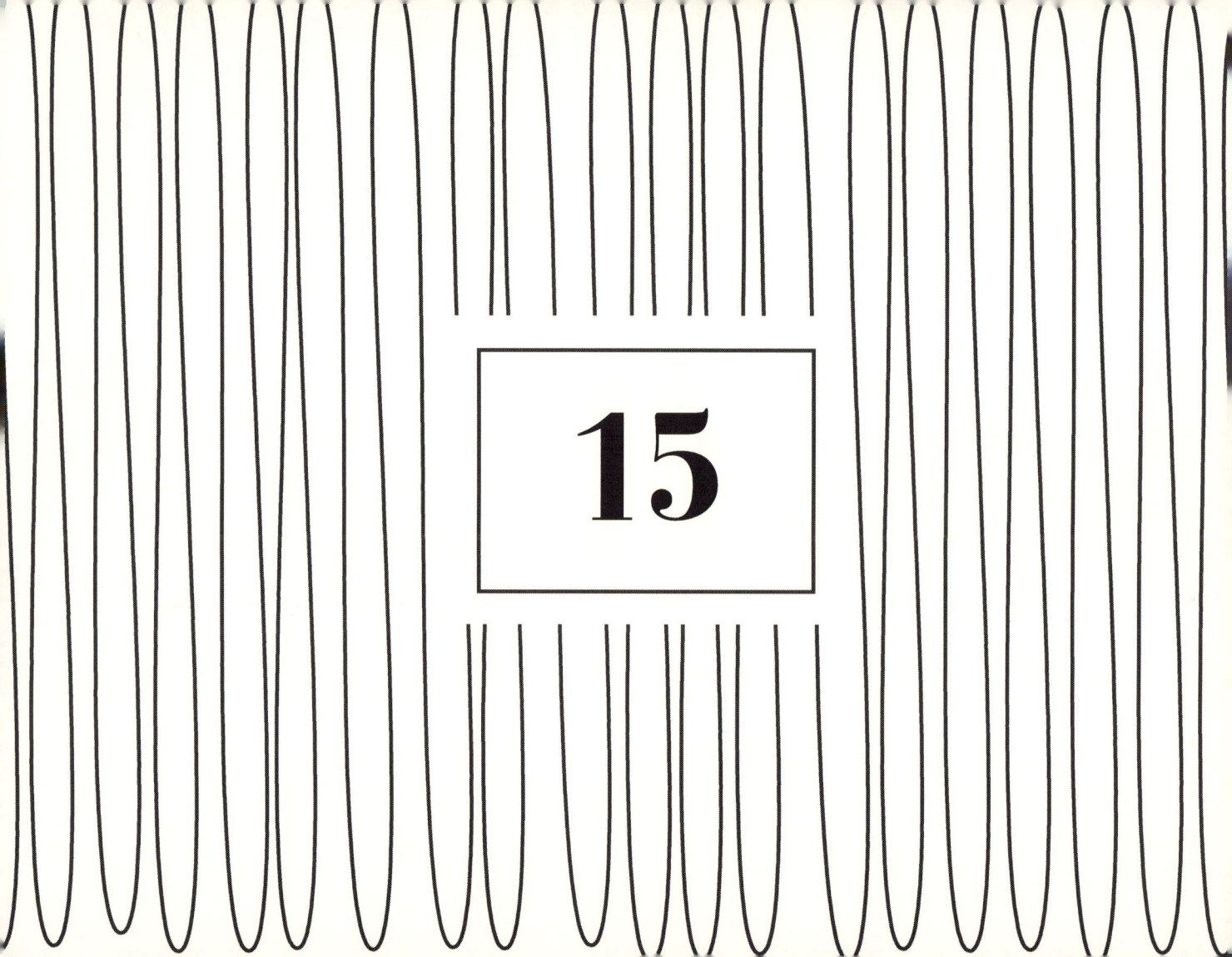

I LOVE HOW YOU NEVER GET TIRED OF _____

I LOVE IT WHEN WE PLAY

---

IF YOU WERE A DESSERT YOU'D BE

_____

18

WHEN YOU LOOK AT ME I FEEL

_____

# 19

MY FAVORITE THING WE'VE DONE WAS

_____

20

I LOVE TO WATCH YOU

_____

**21**

YOU MAKE ME WANT TO BE BETTER AT

_____

**22**

YOU MAKE THE BEST

_____

# 23

ONE WORD TO DESCRIBE YOU IS

_____

24

IF YOU WERE A COLOR YOU'D BE

_____

# 25

I LOVE THAT YOU'RE
MY NAN BECAUSE

_____

## DID YOU ENJOY THIS BOOK?

If so, help others enjoy it too.
Please recommend to friends and
leave a review when possible!

# THERE'S A BOOK FOR EVERYONE YOU LOVE!

| | | |
|---|---|---|
| Grandparents | Parents | My Daughter |
| Grandma | Mom | My Son |
| Nan | My Mommy | My Step Daughter |
| Nana | My Stepmom | My Step Son |
| Nanna | Mum | My Granddaughter |
| Granny | My Mummy | My Grandson |
| Grammy | My Stepmum | My Aunt |
| Gigi | Dad | My Auntie |
| Nonna | My Daddy | My Aunty |
| Mimi | My Stepdad | My Uncle |
| Oma | My Wife | My Nephew |
| Abuela | My Husband | My Niece |
| Grandad | My Boyfriend | |
| Grandpa | My Girlfriend | |
| Pa | My Partner | |
| Pop | My Sister | |
| Papa | My Brother | |
| Opa | Things I Love about You | |
| Nonno | | |

SCAN ME

FIND US ON AMAZON

LOTUS LOVE PRESS

Made in United States
Troutdale, OR
12/27/2023